AF206987

Will Rogers

Native American Star of Stage, Screen, and Politics

by Jennifer Marino Walters
illustrated by Scott R. Brooks

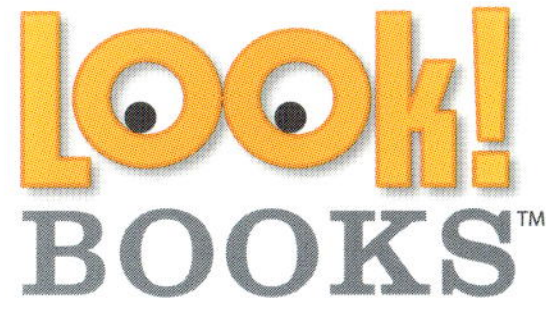

Red Chair Press   Egremont, Massachusetts

Look! Books are produced and published by Red Chair Press:

Red Chair Press LLC   PO Box 333   South Egremont, MA 01258-0333

www.redchairpress.com

 FREE lesson guide at www.redchairpress.com/free-activities

Publisher's Cataloging-In-Publication Data
(Provided by Cassidy Cataloguing Services, Inc.)
Names: Marino Walters, Jennifer, author. | Brooks, Scott R., illustrator.
Title: Will Rogers : Native American star of stage, screen, and politics / by
Jennifer Marino Walters ; illustrated by Scott R. Brooks.

Other titles: Look! books (Red Chair Press). Beginner biography

Description: Egremont, Massachusetts : Red Chair Press, [2024] | Includes
    index. | Interest age level: 006-009. | Summary: Will Rogers, was the
    most famous American entertainer, writer and actor of the early 1900s.
    He was best known for making fun of politics and the U.S. government.
    He is still popular today with politicians in Washington D.C. who praise
    his humor about them.--Publisher.

Identifiers: ISBN: 9781643712536 (library hardcover) | 9781643712598
    (softcover) | 9781643712659 (ebook) | LCCN: 2022943808

Subjects: LCSH: Rogers, Will, 1879-1935--Juvenile literature. | Indian
    entertainers--United States-- Biography--Juvenile literature. |
    Humorists, American--Biography--Juvenile literature. | CYAC: Rogers,
    Will, 1879-1935. | Indian entertainers--United States--Biography. |
    Humorists, American--Biography. | LCGFT: Biographies. | BISAC:
    JUVENILE NONFICTION / Biography & Autobiography / Cultural,
    Ethnic & Regional. | JUVENILE NONFICTION / People & Places
    / United States / Native American. | JUVENILE NONFICTION /
    Performing Arts / Television & Radio.

Classification: LCC: PN2287.R74 M37 2024 | DDC: 792.7/028/092--dc23

Photo credits: Library of Congress

Printed in the United States of America

0324 1P CGF24

Table of Contents

A Young Cowboy

Will Rogers was one of the most famous actors and authors of the 1920s and 1930s. But his life did not begin in the spotlight. Will was born on November 4, 1879 in Oologah, Indian Territory (now Oklahoma). His parents were part Cherokee.

Will earned a Guinness World Record for throwing three lassos at once. One went around a horse's neck, one around the rider, and the third around the horse's legs.

Will grew up on his family's ranch. There, he learned to care for cattle, ride horses, and use a **lasso**. As a teenager, Will worked as a cowboy at various ranches.

The Cherokee Kid

In 1902, Will began to perform in Wild West shows in South Africa and the U.S. He did lasso tricks and rode **broncos** onstage. He soon earned the nickname "the Cherokee kid."

Will also performed his lasso act in variety shows. He often told jokes about politics while doing his tricks. Audiences loved him.

From Stage to Screen

In 1918, Will appeared in his first silent film. When movies began to have sound, he switched to speaking roles. That's when his film career really took off.

In 1933, Will became the highest paid movie star in Hollywood. The following year, he was voted the most popular male actor. In total, he starred in 71 films.

In 1931, Will starred in the comedy film *A Connecticut Yankee* about a trip back in time to King Arthur's Court.

A Mighty Pen

But Will also had other talents. One of them was writing. In 1922, he began to write a weekly newspaper **column** that soon appeared in more than 500 newspapers across the country.

Will Rogers in 1926.

Will also wrote six books.
Several of them became
bestsellers. He became known
for his funny **quips** and his
smart, honest observations about
America and its government.

Spreading His Words

In 1922, Will began to share his thoughts on the radio as well. He landed his own Sunday-evening radio show in 1933. It became a huge hit.

Will also became a popular after-dinner speaker at events. He met and became friends with many important people, including Presidents Calvin Coolidge and Franklin Roosevelt, Thomas Edison, and Charles Lindbergh.

Helping Others

Will used his popularity and success to help others. He donated large amounts of money to charities and disaster-relief efforts. He performed at many events to raise money for various causes. When Oklahoma and other states suffered a **drought** in 1931, Will made more than 50 stops in three days to support victims.

But he always remained **humble**.
"No man is great if he thinks
he is," Will once said.

A Tragic End

Will also had a love for adventure—especially for flying on airplanes. He traveled throughout the world, including all over Europe and South America.

In 1935, Will planned a trip to Alaska with pilot Wiley Post. Sadly, the trip took a tragic turn. On August 15, 1935, the men's plane crashed near Point Barrow, Alaska. Both men died. Will was only 55.

Good to Know

Wiley Post lost one eye in an accident but still learned to fly. In 1934 he designed the first high-altitude pressure suit allowing for future space travel.

A Watchful Eye

But Will still managed to keep his eye on the U.S. government. Before he died, the state of Oklahoma had **commissioned** a statue of Will to be displayed at the U.S. Capitol. Will had agreed to it only if the statue could face the House Chamber so he could keep an eye on Congress.

Good to Know

According to Capitol guides, every U.S. President rubs the left shoe of Will's statue for good luck before entering the House Chamber to give the State of the Union address.

Today, Will's statue is the only one in that part of the Capitol that faces the Chamber entrance.

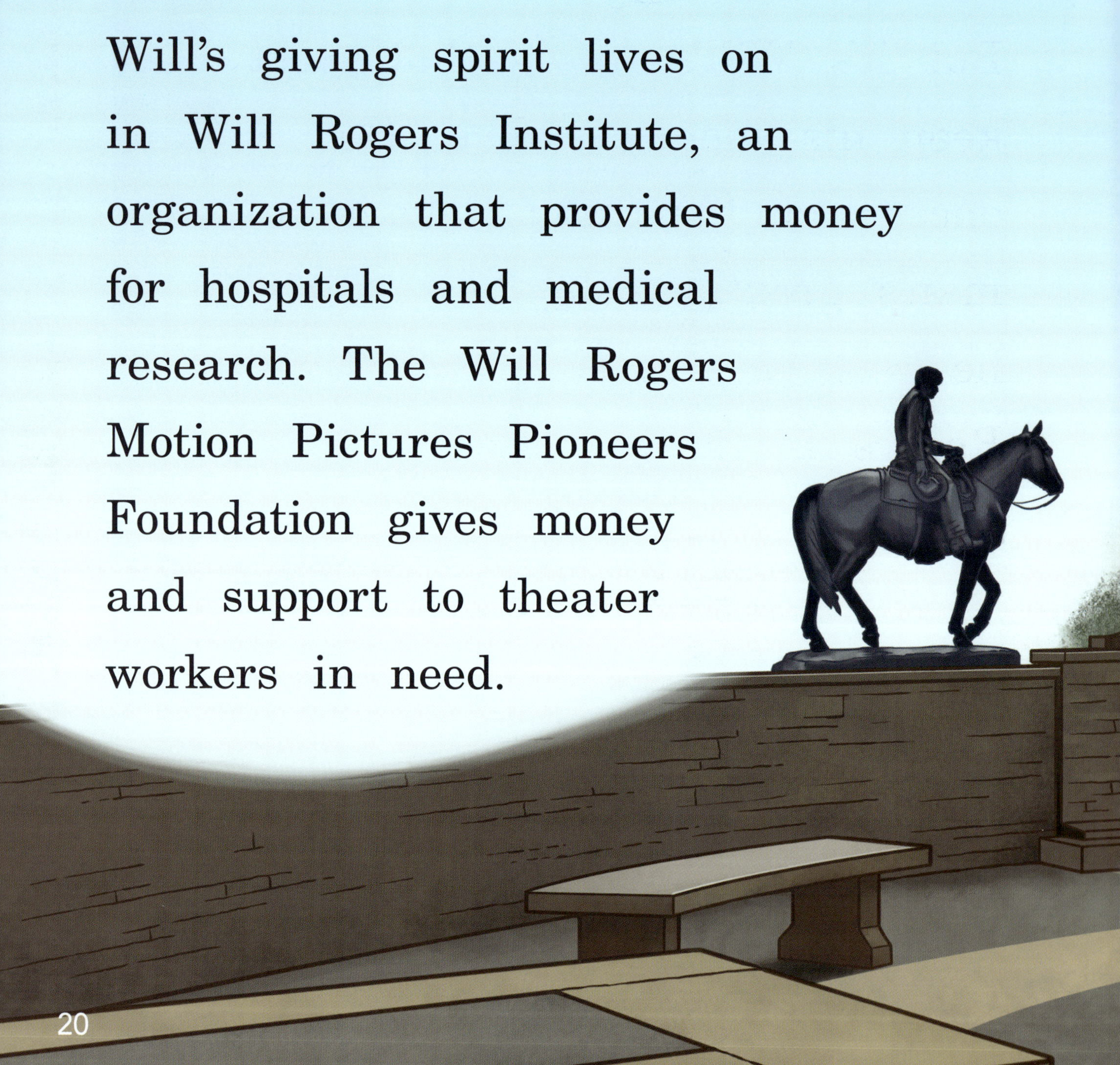

Will's giving spirit lives on in Will Rogers Institute, an organization that provides money for hospitals and medical research. The Will Rogers Motion Pictures Pioneers Foundation gives money and support to theater workers in need.

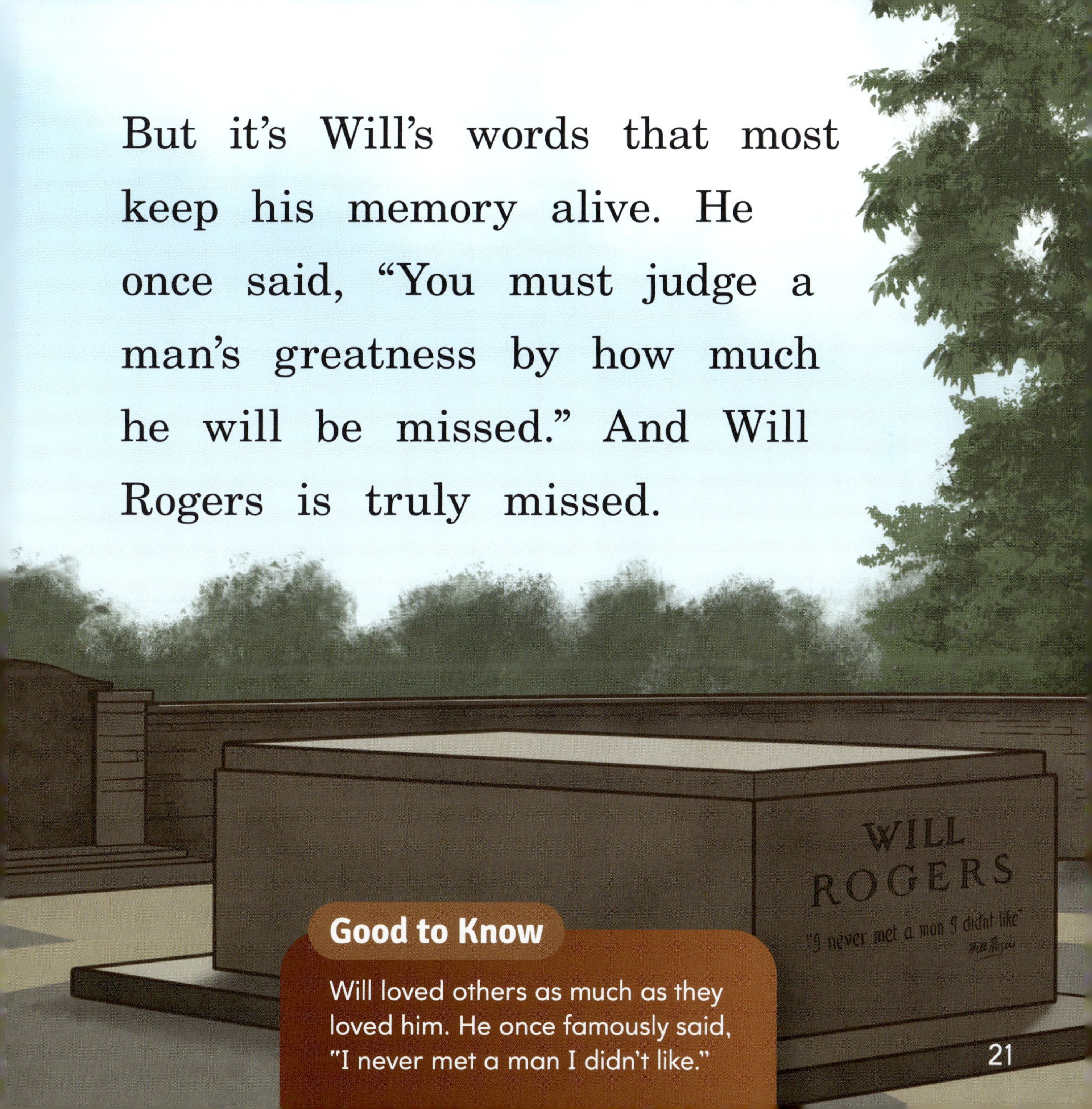

But it's Will's words that most keep his memory alive. He once said, "You must judge a man's greatness by how much he will be missed." And Will Rogers is truly missed.

Good to Know

Will loved others as much as they loved him. He once famously said, "I never met a man I didn't like."

Timeline: Big Dates in Will's Life

1879: Will is born Oologah, Indian Territory (now Oklahoma).

1902: Will begins starring in Wild West shows as a lasso thrower and bronco rider, earning him the nickname "the Cherokee kid."

1908: He marries Betty Blake. They go on to have four children.

1918: Will makes his first motion picture, *Laughing Bill Hyde*.

1922: He begins writing weekly articles that appear in newspapers across the U.S.

1926: Will is elected honorary mayor of Beverly Hills, California.

1929: He makes his first movie with sound.

1933: Will becomes the highest paid movie star in Hollywood and gets his own radio show.

1935: Will is killed in an airplane crash near Point Barrow, Alaska.

1937: Will is buried in a family tomb at the site of his planned retirement ranch in Claremore, Oklahoma. You can visit it at www.willrogers.com

Will Rogers in Hollywood, 1921.

Words to Know

broncos: wild horses of western North America

drought: a long period of time during which there is very little or no rain

commissioned: asked for something to be done

honorary: unofficial

humble: not thinking of oneself as better than other people

lasso: a rope with a loop that is swung and used for catching animals

quips: clever comments

Learn More at the Library

(Check out these books to read with others)

Bailey Beard, Darleen. *Will Rogers: Oklahoma's Favorite Son.* Oklahoma Heritage Association Publishing, 2015.

Keating, Frank. *Will Rogers: Our American Legend.* Oklahoma Hall of Fame, 2018.

Taylor, Bart. *Will Rogers and the Great White House Sleepover.* Yorkshire Publishing, 2021.

Index

About the Author

Jennifer Marino Walters is the author of 20 books for children. She lives with her husband and their twin boys and daughter in the Washington, D.C. area. She has never learned to use a lasso like Will Rogers, but admits it would come in handy when trying to collect her three active children.